Unfuck Your Anxiety Workbook

Faith G. Harper,
PhD, LPC-S, ACS, ACN

Unfuck Your Anxiety Workbook

USING SCIENCE TO REWIRE YOUR ANXIOUS BRAIN

Faith G. Harper,
PhD, LPC-S, ACS, ACN

Microcosm Publishing
Portland, OR

UNFUCK YOUR ANXIETY WORKBOOK

Using Science to Rewire Your Anxious Brain

Part of the 5 Minute Therapy Series

© Dr. Faith Harper, 2021

This edition © Microcosm Publishing, 2021

First edition, first published 2021

ISBN 9781621066835

This is Microcosm #553

Cover by Joe Biel

Edited by Elly Blue

For a catalog, write or visit:

Microcosm Publishing

2752 N Williams Ave.

Portland, OR 97227

503-799-2698

www.Microcosm.Pub

These worksheets can be used on their own, or as a companion to *Unfuck Your Anxiety* by Dr. Faith G. Harper.

These worksheets are free to reproduce but no more than two can be reproduced in a publication without expressed permission from the publisher.

To join the ranks of high-class stores that feature Microcosm titles, talk to your rep: In the U.S. **Como** (Atlantic), **Fujii** (Midwest), **Book Travelers West** (Pacific), **Turnaround** in Europe, **Manda/UTP** in Canada, **New South** in Australia, and **GPS** in Asia, India, Africa, and South America. Sold in the gift market by **Gifts of Nature** and **Faire.**

Did you know that you can buy our books directly from us at sliding scale rates? Support a small, independent publisher and pay less than Amazon's price at www.Microcosm.Pub

Global labor conditions are bad, and our roots in industrial Cleveland in the 70s and 80s made us appreciate the need to treat workers right. Therefore, our books are MADE IN THE USA.

MICROCOSM · PUBLISHING

Microcosm Publishing is Portland's most diversified publishing house and distributor with a focus on the colorful, authentic, and empowering. Our books and zines have put your power in your hands since 1996, equipping readers to make positive changes in their lives and in the world around them. Microcosm emphasizes skill-building, showing hidden histories, and fostering creativity through challenging conventional publishing wisdom with books and bookettes about DIY skills, food, bicycling, gender, self-care, and social justice. What was once a distro and record label was started by Joe Biel in his bedroom and has become among the oldest independent publishing houses in Portland, OR. We are a politically moderate, centrist publisher in a world that has inched to the right for the past 80 years.

TABLE OF CONTENTS

PART II: ADDRESSING YOUR ANXIETY 55

PART III: LIVING WITH YOUR ANXIETY 99

INTRODUCTION

When you struggle with anxiety, the most empowering thing in the world is realizing that you aren't weak, broken, or batshit crazy.

I'm not just saying that to placate you. It's scientifically true. Anxiety makes perfect sense because it's how our brains are wired to protect us. A number of mental health issues, anxiety being one of them, are the direct result of how we have evolved for survival. I go into a lot more depth about this in my books *Unfuck Your Anxiety* and *Unfuck Your Brain*, but here's the short version: Our brains store our most frightening or traumatic memories in a special place and in a special way so we can access them at top-speed. Like I'm asthmatic and keep my rescue inhaler on hand. And just like having a rescue inhaler in my pocket, this is done in order to protect us.

When those memories are triggered, rational thought gets bypassed and our body goes into do something to fix this mode. Even if we're just walking down the street and everything around us is normal. A lot of anxiety is simply our brains keeping us on high alert for threats that are no longer present.

What is anxiety? The American Psychological Association defines it as "an emotion characterized by feelings of tension, worried thoughts and physical changes like increased blood pressure." Maybe a diagnostic starting point, but still undersells the carnival fun house that anxiety really is, so let's go a little deeper, yeah?

The neurocircuitry of anxiety disorders are essentially the same as the human fear circuits. Fear is an emotion designed to motivate us into defensive behaviors based on a specific threat we notice in the environment. The only difference between that and anxiety is that anxiety is responding to a non-specific threat.

There are a ton of areas of the brain associated with a fear response. The amygdala is a big one but parts of the entire brain, prefrontal regions down to specific brain stem nuclei, get involved so we are primed to respond to threats that we have familiarity with (trauma conditioning) and threats that are brand new fuckery that we have never seen before. Short version: We are wired to have strong emotional responses because those responses keep us alive. Feeling anxious is absolutely an important survival skill.

The problem is, the body's stress response is designed to give us a boost of energy to focus our attention on something that is important to our well-being or survival. But modern life is just one big frat party of constant stressors, so it gets turned on regularly or sometimes just... stays on. And that constant stress hormone bombardment can turn into anxiety for many people.

For the purposes of this book, here's how we'll define anxiety:
Anxiety is a state of full body disequilibrium at a level of intensity that demands immediate attention and corrective action on your part. It can be in the face of a real or perceived threat, either present or anticipated. For this workbook, we're going to assume that you are struggling with some form of anxiety, since no one buys anxiety workbooks as a fun and frothy poolside read. You may or may not have been formally diagnosed, but you definitely know it's there, and you are working hard to not have it control your life.

This workbook was developed to go with the book Unfuck Your Anxiety. You can use the books together, or either one on its own. If you want a deeper background into what anxiety is, how it works, and the many conditions it can be related to or mistaken for, Unfuck Your Anxiety has a ton of that. But anything you need to have a good handle on in order to complete these worksheets is included here—you don't have to buy the book for the workbook to make sense, cuz that would be a dick move. If you want more space for any of the exercises, use a notebook. You can also make as many photocopies as you want for your personal use. (If

you want to make copies for your private practice or clients or group,
drop my publisher a line to ask.)

Disclaimer: This book isn't gonna diagnose or treat a medical condition.
There are some helpful questionnaires for finding clinical support.
It's important to have support in your healing, if at all possible. This
workbook is meant to help the process, not replace professional care.

SUDs

Let's start with a metric. I'm pretty sure no one leaves therapy school without the SUDs in their back pocket. SUDS stands for Subjective Units of Distress, and is a scale (usually 0-10 or 0-100 if you wanna get sassy with it) used to measure your intensity of distress. Only you know your insides, and SUDs is the best way (no matter how imperfect) to make that experience known. You're right, it's not an objective measurement like your pulse or vagal tone. Because we aren't focusing on that, we are focusing on how you feel and how it's affecting your ability to do important life shit.

We're going to use SUDs in a bunch of the exercises throughout this book, so go ahead and make notes here about what each level looks and feels like in your experience.

0 = Totally fine. Peaceful and settled in your body, no underlying agitation, upsetness, anxiety, or stress.

1 = Basically okay. Not upset, maybe if you were being super aware you might notice something feels a little unpleasant but it's not a big deal.

2 = A little upset. Maybe not even noticeable if you were busy, but if you're paying attention you would recognize something is bothering you a little.

3 = A little worried, noticing that you're mildly upset.

4 = Upset enough that it isn't easy to ignore. You can handle it, but it definitely doesn't feel good.

5 = Definitely uncomfortable, sorta upset. It feels unpleasant but it's still manageable with effort.

6 = Feeling bad. Recognizing you definitely need to do something about this.

7 = Heading into freak out. Sorta still in control, but almost barely.

8 = This is the official freak out point. No good is coming from this.

9 = Feeling at the edge. Oftentimes a 9 feels a lot like a 10 because you are getting really desperate. You're not at the point of unbearable quite yet, but are very scared that you are losing control and of what may happen.

10 = The worst it has ever felt or could feel. It feels literally unbearable and you feel out of control of your whole personhood.

Grounding Strategies

Grounding may seem like a complicated thing, but in reality all it refers to is our ability to maintain our mental awareness of the here and now. To stay in the present and in our bodies. It's the opposite of dissociation, which is a huge struggle for those of us in trauma recovery.

There are three categories of grounding skills and a billion (or at least several) ideas that fit into each of them. Experiment with at least one new skill every day. I'm adding a few of each to get you started, and endless more are just a google search away.

Mental Grounding	Physical Grounding	Soothing Grounding
Look for three circular items in the room you're in	Run cool water over your wrists	Look at photos or picture someone or something you love
List your favorite movies, music, food, or any other category	Meditate on the soles of your feet	Tell yourself something you would tell your best friend if they were upset

PART 1:

IDENTIFYING

YOUR ANXIETY

Nobody has the same experience of anxiety, so there is no one size fits all treatment approach. How anxiety affects your life is the most important part of figuring out what will help you manage it. These exercises aren't meant to diagnose an Official Anxiety Disorder (no ™), but rather to help you recognize the ways anxiety presents in your life, whether diagnosable levels or not. You don't have to have an official diagnosis to know your own mind, body, and responses better. Then, if you have a treatment provider then *boom* you can bring in your list and say "this is what I need to work on!" and if you don't have a treatment provider at this time you can say "self, this is what we're gonna work on!"

Symptoms of Anxiety

Anxiety is an emotional response that shows itself in mental and very physical ways. Here are some of the things that might look like. Some people might have all these experiences, other people might have a few, or different ones at different times.

You are probably reading the physical body checklist and thinking . . . this is the same list for everything from anxiety to Ebola. Which is why so many people end up in emergency rooms thinking they are having a heart attack when they are having an anxiety attack. It's also the same reason many people have missed the fact that they were having a heart attack because they were also having an anxiety attack. It's important to have any possible medical conditions ruled out because so many physical health issues can look like mental health issues.

For each of these symptoms, put down the SUDs level, 1-10, for how much you experience this symptom in general. You can also record the highest SUDs level you can remember experiencing for this symptom in the last year.

SUDs generally	SUDs recently

Thoughts and Feelings Symptoms

Excessive worry

Rumination (hamster wheel thinking patterns)

Irritability/anger (Weird, right? Anger is the culturally allowed emotion so we substitute that one a lot for what we are really feeling)

Irrational fears/specific phobias

Stage fright/social phobias

Hyper self-awareness/self-consciousness

Feelings of fear

A sense of helplessness

Flashbacks

Obsessive behaviors, pickiness

SUDs generally	SUDs recently

Compulsive behaviors

Self doubt

A sense that you are "losing it" or "going crazy"

Physical Body Symptoms

Trouble falling asleep or staying asleep

Inability to rest

Muscle tension

Neck tension

Chronic indigestion

Stomach pain and/or nausea

Racing heart

Pulsing in the ear (feeling your heartbeat)

Coldness, numbness or tingling in toes, feet, hands, or fingers

Sweating

Weakness

Shortness of breath

Dizziness

Lightheadedness

Chest pain

Feeling hot and cold (feeling like having chills and fever without running a temperature)

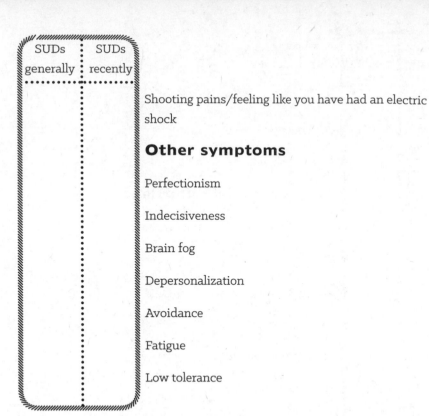

SUDs generally	SUDs recently

Shooting pains/feeling like you have had an electric shock

Other symptoms

Perfectionism

Indecisiveness

Brain fog

Depersonalization

Avoidance

Fatigue

Low tolerance

What are your five most frequent (or strongest or most disruptive) anxiety symptoms? Even if you are thinking, "Hah, all the things!," chances are a few stand out. That way you know what to look for and measure when you try different anxiety management techniques.

1.

2.

3.

4.

5.

Assessing Anxiety

There are lots of assessments for anxiety that clinicians use. The OASIS is the one that is used the most since it's public domain. If you are looking to start a conversation with your healthcare provider about an anxiety diagnosis, this might be a good starting point for you. As in, "Look, I took the OASIS and it was me AF, I'm not trying to get Xanax out of you or anything but I really want to talk about a diagnosis and treatment options."

The OASIS questions ask for you to reflect on your experiences over the past week and rate them on a scale of 0-4, with 0 being no probs, 1 being infrequent, 2 being occasional, 3 being pretty frequent, and 4 being constant fucking companion, thanks for the reminder. Yeah, I'm translating a bit there. You can see the entire scale with the exact wording online, download it and print it if you want. (http://tinyurl.com/jnubjvx) but this is the essential information that the OASIS is looking to collect, plus a few extra questions to help you and your healthcare provider see the patterns that need to be addressed.

In the past week:

How often did you notice that you were feeling anxious?

How did the anxiety present itself? (rapid heartbeat, etc.)

Any particular patterns to the situations that cause anxiety? (taking the bus, having to speak in a group, etc.)

In the past week, when you have felt anxious, how intense or severe was your anxiety on a scale of 1-10? (You can use the SUDs scale here.)

How often did you avoid situations or activities because of your anxiety?

Any patterns in what you avoided?

How much on a scale of 1-10 did your anxiety interfere with your ability to do things you need to do at work, school, stuff around the house, going to appointments, etc?

On a scale of 1-10, how much did your anxiety interfere with your ability to have a social life, enjoy your relationships, or generally have fun?

Is It Anxiety or Stress?

The essential difference between anxiety and stress is whether the pressure we are feeling is internal or external. Anxiety comes from our own internal narrative about what we need to do, should do, are not doing, etc. And stress is the stuff coming into us from other people or events. Anxiety about job performance would be you not thinking you're doing enough, while stress would come from your boss telling you that you aren't doing enough. Of course, you can have stress and anxiety at once, but untangling them can help. Here is a space for you to map out the different internals and externals so you can tailor your approach as needed.

Internal Anxieties	External Stressors

Any connections between how the two columns reinforce each other?

Is It Anxiety or OCD?

While they're both anxiety disorders, generalized anxiety (GAD) and OCD are distinct in some pretty important ways. My book *Unfuck Your Anxiety* goes into some of the science of why OCD is not considered an anxiety disorder. While OCD can also cause significant anxiety, OCD involves different parts of the brain and requires different treatment strategies. There are a few big differences that may help you parse out if OCD is a possible diagnosis for you and your treatment provider to consider. The OCD Center of Los Angeles has a bunch of free online assessments related to OCD and other obsessive disorders, as well!

OCD and anxiety diverge in these three areas. Use the space below each to write out notes to share with your treatment provider:

How extreme are the things that you worry about?

Anxiety, while irrational, tends to be relatively related to life stressors. Like if you have to speak in front of a group, anxiety may tell you that you may pass out or forget how to communicate verbally, while OCD may tell you that you will jump out the window to your death.

How dug-in are the things you worry about?

Anxiety tends to bounce around quite a bit, with a whole host of "what-ifs" to offer you throughout the day. OCD tends to dig in and be present all the time. Like if you are afraid you are going to catch a horrible disease and die or accidently kill someone while riding your bike. These are fears that are not only dug-in, they are often related to your deepest fears as a human being.

Are there any ritual behaviors that you have developed to help soothe these things you are worried about (compulsions)?

Not everyone with OCD has compulsive behaviors. You can have OCD that just involves the first two items in this list, which is often referred to as "pure O" OCD. But if you do have compulsive behaviors, they may be incredibly time consuming and increasingly irrational. For example, worrying about germs during a pandemic turns into so much handwashing that your hands are chapped and increasingly susceptible to germs and bacteria. Or checking the lock on the door 23 times, which makes you consistently late to work. Compulsions don't have to be behavioral, they can also be mental, like saying certain prayers over and over and over to "protect" you from hurting someone, or counting steps so you always end on a certain lucky number, etc.

Make a Trauma-Informed Anxiety Safety Plan

Post-traumatic stress disorder and anxiety co-occur incredibly often. So much so that PTSD used to be categorized as an anxiety disorder, until we got better at parsing out the differences. But since they co-occur so often, having a safety plan that is trauma-informed is super vital for a lot of people. While this safety plan focuses on anxiety, it's designed to consider trauma responses as well.

Not being controlled by your anxiety and trauma responses means being able to recognize when you are safe in the present moment, so let's create your story of safety.

But first, a definition. A trigger is something that facilitates reliving a traumatic event. A trigger is something in the present that activates our past trauma. For example, a car brake squealing can make the brain freak out and make you think that you are getting hit by a car again. Or someone wearing the same scent as an abusive authority figure in your childhood can make all those feelings of anger or helplessness come back. That is your brain warning you that you might be in danger. It doesn't make you crazy, it makes you a survivor.

But it also means you are no longer in the present moment, dealing with present stimuli. It means your brain is playing the tape of whatever terrible shit happened to you in the past as a mechanism of trying to protect you in the present. Your brain just doesn't understand that the present is probably not as scary or dangerous as the recording.

Sometimes we limit ourselves by avoiding all possible triggers, which helps in the short term but not in the long run. And it's also a crappy way to live and you deserve better. Instead, let's work on figuring out what's going on and developing new ways of being so we can live the lives we want for ourselves.

Use the next three exercises to evaluate your triggers and figure out what sets them off and the most effective ways to manage them.

Once you start putting a formal plan into place to manage your triggers, you will notice some stuff works great, some stuff not at all, and new ideas may come up that you want to incorporate. You may also get feedback from the people you love and trust. Make any notes that you want to remember here, too.

When you feel the most healthy, happy, joyful, and well, what does life look like? *Instead of thinking about the absence of a negative emotion, think of the existence of a positive one. How do you feel at these times? How do you interact with others? What do you like to do?*

What things have you noticed help you feel good in these ways? *Getting a certain amount of sleep? Exercise? Eating a certain way, meditating, praying, spending time with people you care about, or meaningful hobbies? What activities work best in your wellness toolbox?*

What are some of the things from this list you can commit to doing on the regular to help you maintain equilibrium? *You don't have to list 97 things. Maybe 1-3 things you aren't doing regularly right now that you know would help.*

What situations activate your anxiety or otherwise act as triggers for you? *These are generally not the big catastrophic things, but things that can happen on a more regular basis. For many people, this can be situations (like being in a crowded room or not doing well on a project), dates (like a holiday or birthday), or something sensory (like a smell or tone of voice). This list can be a work in progress that you keep adding to over time.*

What are your early warning signs that you may be getting anxious, panicky, or otherwise triggered? *What kinds of thoughts do you have? What emotions arise? What kind of behaviors do you engage in that you don't typically do?*

When you notice these signs, what are the things you can do for yourself to help you manage your response to them? *This doesn't mean avoiding everything that causes anxiety! These are often things that you already do for your general wellness, but may also be coping skills or activities that you use when you are in tough situations.*

What support do you need/want/hope to get from others? *While there are a lot of things that you are able to do for yourself, there may be times you need help. Who do you trust to provide that support? How will you ask them for it?*

How will you know that you have been triggered past the point that you can handle? *What will you notice in terms of your behaviors? Your feelings? Your thoughts? What should you and the people who support you watch out for?*

If you are at a point at which you are not able to manage these triggers on your own or with the help of people who traditionally support you, what is the next step? *Do you have treatment professionals who should be contacted? Crisis lines you prefer? A hospital you prefer, if needed? What resources are available to provide additional support?*

Once your crisis has been managed, how will you know when you are feeling safe and secure again? *What does restabilization look like for you? How can you communicate that to the people who may be worried about you?*

Types of Triggers

Both anxiety/panic and trauma have triggers and there is huge overlap between the two for a lot of people. It can be helpful now that we have a plan for these different triggers to go a bit deeper on the types of triggers there are (and you can create a management plan based on those differences).

There are three different ways of being activated by a trigger. Pay attention when you are trauma-activated as to what type of trigger you're experiencing. This information will help you figure out better ways to both manage and recover.

Record your triggers that best match each category:

True Triggers: That pre-thought wordless terror. It's a body based, felt-sense reaction that we often don't even recognize until after the fact. The best way to handle a true trigger is to simply notice its existence and use skills to ground ourselves and bring our bodies back to safety.

Distressing Reminders: These are things that call up memories of the trauma and cause awful feelings but through which we can still think and function. A lot of times we can describe what we are feeling even if we can't explain it. The best way to handle a distressing reminder is to soothe yourself when you are experiencing it.

Uncomfortable Associations: These occur when something that would otherwise be pleasant or at least neutral has an association to our trauma. We are able to manage these associations by consciously reframing them.

Trigger Response Plan

Now that you have an idea about the different types of triggers you are experiencing, you can create a plan to manage them. Practicing coping while you are not being triggered will help you remember what works when you need to. Try using coping and grounding skills from the introduction exercises that are specific to your types of triggers and rate how they worked so you can start to develop a more specific plan of attack for dealing with them.

True Triggers

Trigger	Coping Skill	Effectiveness

Distressing Reminders

Trigger	Coping Skill	Effectiveness

Uncomfortable Associations

Trigger	Coping Skill	Effectiveness

Your Anxiety Narrative

We all experience anxiety in different ways. We are the product of our experiences, and the crappy ones tend to dig into our brains far more easily than the lovely ones. What has happened to us, what we have witnessed, what we were taught by others. Being more mindful of our own experiences of anxiety is the first part in recognizing our own unique experiences. And that allows us a better understanding of them (brain science!) and then managing them (therapy hacks!).

What incident from your past that you have not let go of has the biggest hold on you?

What situations typically trigger anxiety for you on a day-to-day basis?

What does your anxiety look like (how do you behave when anxious)?

Which of your behaviors fuel your anxiety and make it worse?

What sensations do you feel in your body when anxious?

How does your anxiety affect your day to day life?

How has anxiety been destructive to your relationships?

How has it been self-destructive?

Is there anyone in your past that you learned your anxiety behavior from?

In what ways does your anxiety continue to serve you?

In what ways does it operate as a barrier?

What would life be like if you were not so anxious?

Would working through your anxiety be worthwhile? How?

Feelings

Our emotions (also known as our feelings) are very similar to our thoughts but can be harder to pin down. And if we deal with anxiety on a constant basis, it's so overwhelming that anything else going on underneath tends to go unnoticed. But these other feelings could be what's activating the anxiety. Or they could be symptoms of other issues that also need your attention and care. Since a thought is just something that your brain tells you, you already know the words to use. But emotions are a different form of communication from inside our bodies and brains, so we have to learn the language to describe them.

Here is a list to get you started, but you can also search online for a "feelings wheel" or add your own to this list.

Joy	Playfulness
Frustration	Boredom
Anger	Shame
Sadness	Envy
Amusement	Jealousy
Confusion	Irritation
Annoyance	Courage
Excitement	Fear
Satisfaction	Confidence
Coziness	Loving
Disappointment	Vulnerability
Despair	Nervousness
Surprise	Contentment
Anxiety	Curiosity

Feelings Identification

In this exercise we will tease out the physical, visual, and mental manifestations of your primary emotions. Next to each dot, list an emotion that you frequently experience. Then list everything that you associate with that emotion. Feel free to start with anxiety, that's the big one you are working on right now...

But don't forget the other ones! E.g. "When I'm angry, I think that everyone has betrayed me and I want to smash things. People notice that my face tenses and keep their distance."

By each dot below, list an emotion and then make some notes about how you know that you are experiencing these emotions.

You will often feel a disconnect or a betrayal between your body and your mind as values from your upbringing are instilling feelings that you don't want to have because they aren't consistent with how you see the world now. If you were taught that you should always respect authority figures but one routinely insults you, your feelings will tell you when your actions are not in line with your values. Sit with your feelings and process what is going on in your body and mind. This is how you work them out of your life. What are some examples of this in your life now?

Make a list of events or behaviors that frequently cause those emotions, rating each one 1-10 on the scale of unpleasantness, using the SUDs scale from the first exercise.

What do you appreciate or need when experiencing each feeling? What is the useful information?

WEEKLY MOOD TRACKER

MOOD OR...
DO YOU SUCK?

	MOOD	SITUATION	MAGNITUDE (0–100)	SYMPTOMS
SUNDAY				
MONDAY				
TUESDAY				
WEDNESDAY				
THURSDAY				
FRIDAY				
SATURDAY				

WEEKLY MOOD TRACKER

	MOOD	SITUATION	MAGNITUDE (0–100)	SYMPTOMS
SUNDAY				
MONDAY				
TUESDAY				
WEDNESDAY				
THURSDAY				
FRIDAY				
SATURDAY				

WEEKLY MOOD TRACKER

MOOD OR...
DO YOU SUCK?

	MOOD	SITUATION	MAGNITUDE (0-100)	SYMPTOMS
SUNDAY				
MONDAY				
TUESDAY				
WEDNESDAY				
THURSDAY				
FRIDAY				
SATURDAY				

WEEKLY MOOD TRACKER

	MOOD	SITUATION	MAGNITUDE (0-100)	SYMPTOMS
SUNDAY				
MONDAY				
TUESDAY				
WEDNESDAY				
THURSDAY				
FRIDAY				
SATURDAY				

WEEKLY MOOD TRACKER

AM I IN A BAD MOOD OR... DO YOU SUCK?

	MOOD	SITUATION	MAGNITUDE (0–100)	SYMPTOMS
SUNDAY				
MONDAY				
TUESDAY				
WEDNESDAY				
THURSDAY				
FRIDAY				
SATURDAY				

Somatic Experience of Anxiety

Like most mental health or emotional things, anxiety is very physical. Use the outlines below to draw or color what you feel in your body when you're anxious or panicking, and where. You can use colors or textures to denote intensity, or just write in the words. If you use colors, make a note of what the colors represent for you! You can also write SUDs numbers in here to indicate the intensity of the sensations.

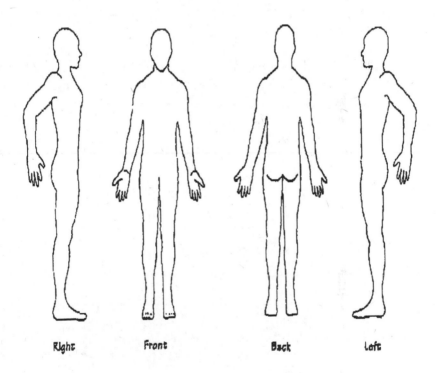

Right   Front   Back   Left

Personal Symptom Record

Anxiety, depression, and mood disorders don't show up on lab tests. To get help for them, you'll usually need to get your own damn self into a clinic or doctor's office saying "shit is fucked and I really really need to figure this out and get help" so that someone can help you sort through the shit and figure out what's wrong. And that's what this worksheet is for. Not for you to self-diagnose and then demand Xanax from your doc, but for you to take time to create a good record of what's been going on so you can connect with a clinician who can ask good questions, clarify information, and help you figure out what treatment and support you need... and hopefully in far less than ten fucking years. So consider using this and bringing it in to your appointment and requesting to go through it with your treatment provider.

What does "symptom" mean? Anything that you are thinking, feeling, or doing that is reinforcing problems or stuckness in your life instead of growth and healing.

Symptom	Intensity (1-10)	How long does it last?	How many times per week?	For how many months/years?

Panic Attack Log

Some people with anxiety get panic attacks, which is when your body's survival instincts go haywire in an attempt to protect you. Many people live with anxiety and it's not super obvious that they're anxious, while panic attacks always use their outside voice. Unlike "regular" anxiety, panic attacks come on quickly, sometimes without warning. Symptoms can include chest pain, heart racing or pounding, nausea, shortness of breath, dizziness, shaking, chills or hot flashes, sweating, numbness or tingling, feelings of choking or unreality, fears of losing control, going insane, or dying. The treatment strategies for dealing specifically with panic attacks come from the developers of "Mastery of your Anxiety and Panic" (MAP, developed by David H. Barlowe and Michelle G. Craske). These next worksheets are based on their model, and their whole workbook may be a good investment for you if panic attacks are currently ruling your life.

We'll give you room to log a few here. If you find this helpful, you can make copies or use a notebook to keep track for a longer time.

Panic Attack #1

Day/date: Time began: Duration:

Expected/Anticipated: ☐   Out of Nowhere: ☐

Where was I? What was I doing? Who was I with?:

What triggered the attack?:

Highest level of fear: 1 2 3 4 5 6 7 8 9 10

Symptoms I experienced:

What I was thinking during the attack:

What I did during the attack:

Were any of these behaviors helpful? How so?

Did any of these behaviors make it worse? How so?

What I did to take care of myself afterwards:

Was this self-care helpful? In what ways?

What else might have been helpful, upon reflection?

Panic Attack #2

Day/date: Time began: Duration:

Expected/Anticipated: ☐   Out of Nowhere: ☐

Where was I? What was I doing? Who was I with?:

What triggered the attack?:

Highest level of fear: 1 2 3 4 5 6 7 8 9 10

Symptoms I experienced:

What I was thinking during the attack:

What I did during the attack:

Were any of these behaviors helpful? How so?

Did any of these behaviors make it worse? How so?

What I did to take care of myself afterwards:

Was this self-care helpful? In what ways?

What else might have been helpful, upon reflection?

Panic Attack #3

Day/date: Time began: Duration:

Expected/Anticipated: ☐   Out of Nowhere: ☐

Where was I? What was I doing? Who was I with?:

What triggered the attack?:

Highest level of fear: 1 2 3 4 5 6 7 8 9 10

Symptoms I experienced:

What I was thinking during the attack:

What I did during the attack:

Were any of these behaviors helpful? How so?

Did any of these behaviors make it worse? How so?

What I did to take care of myself afterwards:

Was this self-care helpful? In what ways?

What else might have been helpful, upon reflection?

Track Your Panic

As you keep track of your panic attacks, being able to see the big picture can help. When you are still dealing with shit on the regular, it can be difficult to see how your hard work is paying off and that things really are getting better. A couple of panic attacks in one week does feel super overwhelming, until you see that they used to be a daily occurrence. Then you realize you are a badass doing amazing work.

And? You may also see that there are patterns to your symptoms that give you some insight on how to better support yourself. Maybe there are certain times of the week, month, or year that you're more likely to have panic attacks. Or they mainly hit you on days that you meet with your boss, or certain anniversaries.

You can use a calendar or an app or make a spreadsheet to track this if you're a digital rockstar that way. Or you can act as middle-aged as I am and pull out your colored pencils and use this chart to track them for a couple some months and see what happens.

For each day, write in the number of panic attacks you have. (If you usually only have 1 or fewer a day, you can write the level of severity instead for days you have one.) Then color code the days based on how much anxiety you experienced in general that day: Red for a ton, orange for medium, yellow for some, and green for chill. (Or come up with your own color scheme, I don't want to harsh your creativity vibe.)

Day 1	Day 2	Day 3	Day 4	Day 5	Day 6	Day 7

PART II: ADDRESSING YOUR ANXIETY

C hances are, anxiety isn't a new thing in your life. It's been problematic for a minute and has felt hopeless and overwhelming. So I want to talk a little bit about the difference between knowledge, abilities, and skills. Stay with me, it's relevant. Knowledge is our intellectual understanding of something. It's an important component to getting better, but doesn't translate into action in and of itself. Understanding the "but why" helps you make changes, but we all know people who are well aware of their bullshit and aren't doing anything about it.

This is where ability and skill come in. Skills are our proficiencies. The things that either other people teach us (training) or we learn through experience (self-training through doing dumb shit and learning better). Abilities are our qualities of being able to do something. It's our innate ability to learn things, to make changes, to hustle on our own behalf.

Someone may have an innate ability to be an amazing musician. But they need the knowledge of why breathing is important and then the skills training on breathwork and the like to harness their full vocal range. We've been building a ton of knowledge, and now we are moving on to the skills part. But I also want you to think about the innate abilities you have to put these into action. No matter how tamped down or smashed out you feel over the years as part of the process of surviving other traumatic events and other life curveballs.

Those natural abilities are still there and ready to shine. I want you to think about how you learn best and how you perform best. So you can take on and build these skills based on those abilities. This is a huge part of why I include a lot of different tools in every book and workbook, you have to try them on and see which are best for your own operating system. Anxiety as a part of your life may or may not get better, but you can definitely get better at it and reclaim the good shit again. So let's get some new skills!

Personify That Asshole

Give your anxiety an actual persona to inhabit. Name it after a heinous ex, a shitty grade school teacher, or Kim Jong-un. Create a whole character for your anxiety. Anxiety feels so nebulous that giving yourself someone or something to battle really helps. Then when anxiety comes calling, you can focus on that entity the way you would an actual person that was threatening you in a real-world situation. You can negotiate, you can yell back, you can lock it in a box. Whatever works. Here's an outline for you to start with, but if your anxiety comes in a non-human shape, don't let this limit you!

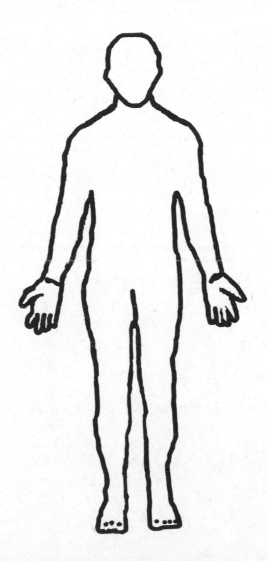

Coping Cards

Coping statements are pretty much as simple as they sound: Mantras or reminders that help you manage your anxiety and stay in control of your body. They can be literal self-talk ("This will only last a minute") or a reminder to take a deep breath. You know, whatever helps. But the problem with coping statements is you sure as fuck aren't going to remember them in the heat of the moment. When you find mantras, facts about anxiety, or other statements or images that help you, put them on an index card. Hole punch those and put them on a snap-shut key ring and you have a set of coping cards you can flip through when panic hits. It sounds epically nerdy, I know. But I have had so many clients end up loving the shit out of their cards and using them all the time.

Some sample states for the cards:

• "This situation doesn't deserve any more of my time than it has already taken."

• "This isn't about me and I don't have to take ownership of it."

• "I am not my anxiety"

• "This is not an actual emergency, I've dealt with far worse."

• "I'm so focused on the negative, I'm forgetting the positive, including..."

• Reach out to a friend I trust for connection

• Make tea

• Take a walk

• Extend out my outbreath to calm my nervous system

• Plan a fun event to look forward to in the next few days

Ride the Wave

Avoidance always makes anxiety worse. Instead of fighting back when you start to get anxious, try setting aside 5 minutes to sit with it. It won't last forever, I swear on my Roomba it won't. If you attend to what you are feeling, you get over it way more quickly than if you avoid it. I've noticed I'm bored with myself about 3 minutes into committing to sitting with my anxiety for 5. I'm ready to go make a cup of coffee, read a book, find the cookies I hid from myself, or do anything other than perseverate.

As you sit with your anxiety, you'll notice it often comes in waves (this is different from panic attacks, which come on very suddenly). After your next bout of anxiety, use the worksheet below to describe the wave—what ongoing situation led up to it, what triggered the anxiety, what happened when it peaked, how you came out of it, and what state you went back to when you felt more in control again. Add your SUDs level for every stage.

Stressors: (Eg, my relationship with my father)

Triggers: (Eg, he didn't follow through with something he promised)

Peak: (Name your emotions at the peak of the anxiety wave. Eg, I felt angry at everyone around me, totally out of control. My heart was racing and my stomach hurt)

Recovery: (Eg, Once my anxiety went down, so did my anger. I felt totally exhausted and guilty, and cried)

Control: (Eg, the situation hasn't changed, but I don't feel as upset about it.)

Now that you're past the wave and feeling more in control of your emotions, look back and examine it further:

Factors that increased the anxiety: (Eg, my stepmother calling)

Factors that supported me: (Eg, I called a friend)

Coping skills I could have used to prevent the wave: (Eg, taking a time out or finding a distraction)

Coping skills that helped me come down from the peak: (Eg, going for a fast walk)

Learned Optimism

Some people are naturally optimistic. Others are hardwired for negativity, which probably kept us alive in the past. Moving on, retraining ourselves for optimism, is good for our emotional health. This worksheet is inspired by Martin Seligman's positive psychology, which is discussed in more depth on chapter 6 of *Unfuck Your Brain*. The idea is to catch your negative thinking habits and retrain your brain.

You can do this as often as you want, but try to do it at least once a week.

Learned Optimism Log Directions:

Your first time, just fill out the first three categories (A-B-C). At the end of that period go back and look for examples of pessimism and negativity. Highlight those instances. Did you beat yourself up way more than you expected?

For the second go round, add the last categories (A-B-C-D-E). This is gonna be harder—this is active work to challenge that pessimism and teach yourself optimism instead. But you got this, rock star. It takes practice, stick with it!

1. **Adversity:** Just the facts, baby. Describe what happened (who, what, where, when) being as precise and detailed as you can.

2. **Beliefs:** What were you thinking? Like, exactly. What was your self-talk? Don't care if it was crude, ugly, or weird. Write it down. If it sparked a memory or flashback, that counts, too!

3. **Consequences:** How did these thoughts effect how you felt? How you behaved? What went on in your body? What emotions did you experience? How did you react?

4. **Dispute:** There are four different ways you can dispute these negative beliefs

a. **Evidence?** Is there evidence that your belief was based in reality? If someone says "I hate you," then the belief that they hate you has some evidence behind it, right? But most beliefs really don't.

b. Alternatives? Is there another way you can look at this situation? What were the non-static circumstances (for instance, do you really always bomb tests, or were you tired this time from being sick?)? What are the specifics (for instance, maybe you lost a basketball game, but does that make you a bad human being or even a bad athlete)? What did others contribute to the situation (is whatever happened really ALL your fault)?

c. Implications? Is the situation really a total catastrophe? What's some perspective you can add to this (ok, so you didn't get that job...does that really mean no one will hire you from now to infinity)?

d. Usefulness? Just because something is true doesn't make it useful. How can you frame the experience as one that gives meaning to your life? Do you have a better respect for those things or people you value? Can you better demonstrate that respect now?

5. Energization: How do you feel post-disputation? Did your behavior change? Your feelings? Did you notice anything within the problem that you didn't notice before? Maybe even created a solution?

Here's a place to practice your learned optimism by keeping track of how you responded to bad or stressful things that happened. These "adverse events" could be anything from big, like losing your job, to relatively minor like getting frustrated by a confusing bill.

Now go celebrate your success here, hot stuff!

LEARNED OPTIMISM LOG

ADVERSE EVENT

Adversity

Belief

Consequences

Disputation

- *Evidence?*

- *Alternatives?*

- *Implications?*

- *Usefulness?*

Energization

LEARNED OPTIMISM LOG

ADVERSE EVENT

Adversity

Belief

Consequences

Disputation

- Evidence?

- Alternatives?

- Implications?

- Usefulness?

Energization

LEARNED OPTIMISM LOG

ADVERSE EVENT

Adversity

Belief

Consequences

Disputation

• *Evidence?*

• *Alternatives?*

• *Implications?*

• *Usefulness?*

Energization

LEARNED OPTIMISM LOG

ADVERSE EVENT

Adversity

Belief

Consequences

Disputation

• *Evidence?*

• *Alternatives?*

• *Implications?*

• *Usefulness?*

Energization

LEARNED OPTIMISM LOG

ADVERSE EVENT

Adversity

Belief

Consequences

Disputation

• Evidence?

• Alternatives?

• Implications?

• Usefulness?

Energization

Cognitive Defusion

A lot of our experience of anxiety can come from internal judgments of ourselves that we may not even notice ourselves believing. One of the best tools from Acceptance and Commitment Therapy reframes our emotional responses through a technique called defusion. Defusion is the process of recognizing our thoughts and feelings as something we have rather than something that we are. Let's try it with some of the main critical meta-messages you have held about yourself:

My mind tells me I am too much of _____

My mind tells me I am not enough of _____

My mind tells me I do too much of _____

My mind tells me I do not do enough of _____

My mind tells me I lack _____

Now take this list and sit with it for a half a minute or so as something you are. Write it down, and even say out loud to yourself:

I am too awkward.

I am too lazy.

I don't move fast enough.

I am not _____

I am too _____

I lack _____

I can't _____

I shouldn't _____

Check in with yourself. How do you feel in your body after just half a minute of taking ownership of these thoughts?

Now try a shift out of judgement, by labeling it as a thought that exists, not something that you are.

I'm noticing that I'm having a thought about being too awkward.

I'm noticing that I am having a thought about being lazy.

I'm noticing that I am having a thought that I do not move fast enough.

I'm noticing that I am having a thought about being_____

I'm noticing that I am having a thought about not being_____

I'm noticing that I am having a thought about being too _____

I'm noticing that I am having a thought about not being able to _____

_____

I'm noticing that I am having a thought about_____

I'm noticing that I am having a thought about_____

I'm noticing that I am having a thought about_____

All defusion means (and yeah, sorry for the term . . . we like to create words for concepts to confuse as many people as possible) is that you are separating your self-ness out of your thoughts and noticing them as something that exists rather than something you are.

Check in with yourself again. How does your body feel when you are no longer fused with these thoughts as indicative of your self-hood?

Having a GOOD Mindset

Stress isn't in and of itself bad—it's not necessarily a problem you need to solve or get away from. This is borne out by multiple studies, including one where the researchers found that just saying "I'm excited" out loud can reappraise stress as excitement. Despite what most of us have been told, it's easier for the brain to jump from anxious feelings to excited ones rather than calm ones.

The practice of reframing our thoughts from those of overwhelm to those of empowerment is known as mindset training. This doesn't mean bullshitting ourselves, but recognizing that we do have the capacity to handle tough situations, or at least the capacity to give it our all and try our best. This isn't negating the fact that we may be dealing with really fucked up situations, but is about taking back whatever power we have in our own responses when dealing with shitshow scenerios.

Mindset training has a direct impact on our stress response. One study found that a stronger physical stress response was associated with higher test scores in school situations, but only for people who have had mindset training. Another study demonstrated that just by telling people "You're the kind of person whose performance improves under pressure" increases their task performance by 33%. One of the biggest predictors of stress overwhelming us is our perception of not being up to the task, so focusing on the fact that we are, indeed, up to it shifts our thinking.

And yes, individuals with anxiety can absolutely benefit from mindset training. Since stress is one of the biggest anxiety triggers, researchers have demonstrated that the stress response (at least the beginnings of it) is the same for people who have anxiety and those who do not. It's our perception of what it means that differs. So a disruption of that stress response can end up circumventing anxiety and panic attacks.

You can practice mindset training as part of your daily self-care routine. I like the GOOD acronym of mindset training since it doesn't involve any kind of fake hype about shitty situations, it really just is about being grounded in your own self-efficacy. And clearly you are a fucking survivor—you're reading this right now, which means your survival rate thus far is 100%, right?

This is one of those internal work exercises that might be easier to make external by journaling through it, especially at first while you get used to the process.

Gratitude: Focusing on gratitude is a really good part of our mental health in general and can create a perspective shift in our day. This doesn't mean discounting what's problematic, but focusing more on what's good in your life.

Today I am grateful for:

Openness to Possibilities: If we are gratitude focused, we are far more likely to be aware of solutions, support, and opportunities around us. In a negative mindset, we are more likely to dismiss things that are available to us (or not notice them at all) because we are overwhelmed and frustrated with life in general.

Today I choose to be open to:

Opportunities in this Experience: No matter what experience we are having, we can focus on the opportunities that exist to help us grow. We can learn more about different situations and ourselves even if we don't achieve the success we were hoping for.

Today I recognize the opportunities to:

Determine: Visualize yourself successfully embracing the challenges ahead. This is hardiness in action. If you mentally set yourself up for success, you are in the right frame of mind to tackle the project. And no, you aren't more frustrated if things don't go perfectly.

Today success looks like:

What About When You Didn't?

In therapy-speak, we call this an exception-seeking question. Meaning, let's look at the times that you didn't manage anxiety badly. Sometimes the best tools already lie within you. We just need to figure out how you draw upon those tools on the regular.

Can you think of a time where you were anxious and you didn't let it take you over?

How did you do it?

What was different?

What helped?

The Bigger Picture

Think about a current or upcoming event or decision that your anxiety likes to hook into. The brain likes to rehearse for the worst case outcome so it isn't taken by surprise if it happens. It doesn't quite work that way, but it's still going to be our first line of thought. So in order to keep a more balanced perspective, you can use this tool to balance your approach and recognize that there are not only negative outcomes all the time. This gives you a chance to widen out from the worst possible scenario to other more positive and more probable outcomes. To gain this perspective, ask yourself: What is the best outcome? What is the absolute worst thing that could happen? What is the most likely thing to happen?

For example, say you're getting bored with your job and are trying to decide whether or not to look for a new one. Best outcome: the first one you apply for will be your dream job and you'll be immediately hired, have supportive bosses, colleagues, and mentors, and eventually become the best CEO the company has ever had. Worst case: your boss finds out you're looking for a new job, fires you, and you lose your apartment, and one day your ex walks by as you're panhandling and mocks you while an atomic bomb speeds towards your city. Most likely scenario? You'll put out some feelers, have an awkward talk with your boss, and suffer a few rejections before you eventually either move into a better role in your current job or find another job that better suits you.

Decision or event I'm struggling with:

What is the best possible outcome?

What is the absolute worst possible outcome?

What is most likely to happen?

You may be thinking "yeah, but...." And, okay. What if the worst thing ever happens? Sometimes it does, I recognize. But you have a 100% survival rate thus far. What strategies would you use to manage a shitty outcome?

Thoughts as Guesses

As mentioned in the previous exercise, anxiety's goal is to prepare you for possible problems (thanks, fucker). One good trick for managing that from the MAP folks is to treat the thoughts as guesses, rather than predetermined outcomes (this is another way to keep us from getting fused with our thoughts). For every catastrophe guess, try coming up with as many other guesses as you can. You don't have to be all sunshine and roses and only say things like "everything will be amazing," you're just looking for a space between disaster stone and perfect outcome.

Catastrophic guess: _____

Other guesses:

- _____

- _____

- _____

- _____

Catastrophic guess: _____

Other guesses:

- _____

- _____

- _____

- _____

Catastrophic guess: _____

Other guesses:

- _____

- _____

- _____

- _____

Vitality vs. Suffering

Your actions can affect your anxiety and other feelings more than you may think. This exercise is a tool from ACT (Acceptance and Commitment Therapy) that's designed to help you create more informed coping strategies.

Look back on the last time a painful thought, feeling, urge, sensation, or memory arose for you. What did you do in response? Write it all down. Now circle "V" next to actions that increased your vitality, improving your well-being, health, relationships, finances, or life generally (eg, you took some deep breaths and called your best friend). And circle the "S" next to actions that increased your suffering, draining the life force from you and those around you (eg, you yelled at your coworker and ate the entire bag of cheetos). After you keep track for a while, you may start to notice patterns, or at least be able to add to your list of go-to coping skills.

Painful thought/feeling: _____

What I did in response:

- _____

- _____

- _____

- _____

Painful thought/feeling: _____

What I did in response:

- _____

- _____

- _____

- _____

Self Empathy and Needs

When we're dealing with anxiety, we often tend to label our emotions in some kind of binary. Good or bad, right or wrong, wanted or unwanted. There's a fuck-ton of problems associated with doing so however. Any negative labels lead us to trying to resist, or suppress, or transform those emotions. Or beat ourselves up for having them.

When we are being mindful of our emotions, on the other hand, we just notice them with curiosity instead of labeling them in a positive or negative category. As in "Oh, I'm feeling _____. I wonder where that is coming from? I wonder what that's about? Is that emotion connected to something I'm not getting that I need?"

For this exercise, reflect on a difficult or painful feeling you recently experienced. Maybe you started to feel panicky before you left for work in the morning. Where did that come from? Was it related to a situation at home, at work, or along your commute? What unmet needs are at play in this situation? Is your safety at stake? Are you feeling disconnected or unsupported? Do you just need some space?

Difficult feeling: _____

Where is this feeling coming from?

What unmet needs might this feeling be connected to?

Difficult feeling: _____

Where is this feeling coming from?

What unmet needs might this feeling be connected to?

Self Sabotage Worksheet

Sometimes we are so afraid of failing that we set ourselves up to do so. If you engage in self-sabotage, you probably know it. Let's get to the bottom of it.

In what ways do you undermine yourself?

Describe your thoughts, feelings, and emotions at these times.

Is there a pattern?

Where did these behaviors come from?

What can you commit to doing to change these behaviors?

What Is In My Control?

Sometimes our anxiety, worries, and stress feel out of control because they elicit such strong reactions in our body . . . and because we are focused on the aspects of the situation that actually are outside of our control. Worrying about things we have no influence over gives our brains a false sense that we are doing something about them, rather than shifting our focus on the aspects of the situation where we do have some control. Stepping back and figuring out what has us stuck in an unproductive loop can help to get some clarity about what we can't do so that we can be free to focus on what we can do.

We're drawing a distinction here between control and influence—control means things that you have entire ownership of, whereas influence is stuff that you are likely to be able to impact by communicating and behaving as effectively as possible.

For your biggest anxiety or worry, break out your concerns and potential actions into three spheres.

My biggest concern: _____

Outside my power

What and who I can influence

What I can control

Thinking Errors

We all have habits of thought that get us into trouble (because brains are asshooooooles). This is the list of thinking errors from my depression book, although thinking errors can cause all kinds of mood problems, not just depression. Pay attention to which thinking errors have become your biggest habit, and brainstorm some alternatives that you can consciously use instead of getting stuck in your old thinking patterns.

For each thinking error, note down some examples of when you've thought that way, and try to come up with a more helpful alternative thought. Alternative doesn't mean sugarcoating it or lying to yourself. For instance, the thought "My mom doesn't love me enough to get clean so she can get custody of me" is hard to switch to "My mom loves me so much and is working so hard," because not true. But "My mom's demons don't represent my value and loveableness" is a more helpful alternative that is still true.

Polarized Thinking: This is as black and white as a yin-yang symbol. Everything gets categorized as either good or bad. Then there is no middle ground. Which means if you aren't completely perfect, you must be a total failure.

Times I think this way:

More helpful alternative thoughts:

Overgeneralization: This takes polarized thinking to a whole new level. It's your brain taking one example of something that happened one time and deciding this is how things are going to roll forever. So if you have failed at something, you are a failure and will continue to be so for time eternal. So why even bother trying?

Times I think this way:

More helpful alternative thoughts:

Mind Reading: This is where you decide you know without a doubt why people are acting the way they act, saying what they say, and what they are thinking and feeling. Huge-ass leaps to conclusions. This is a lot of times based on projection. We know how we are thinking and feeling and presume that others would think and feel the same. Or we feel so shitty about ourselves that we presume others must have the same opinion of us.

Times I think this way:

More helpful alternative thoughts:

Personalization: So we all have the tendency to be the star of our own personal movie, right? And if we are the star, then everything going on around us must relate to us, right? So we are mind reading other people's intent as being about us instead of about them and presume that the ways they respond are due to something negative about us.

Times I think this way:

More helpful alternative thoughts:

Control Fallacies: Fallacies of control fuck you up in either direction. If you feel totally controlled by everything around you, then you are totally a helpless victim. If you feel that you have to be in control of everything all the time, you feel responsible for everything all of the time. Neither is an empirical truth. Both extremes set you up for failure and exhaustion.

Times I think this way:

More helpful alternative thoughts:

Fallacy of Fairness: I was pretty damn young when my mom told me, in essence, that life wasn't fair and I was exhausting myself by expecting it to be. If you are keeping a running fairness tally, you are going to be resentful or pissed off all the time.

Times I think this way:

More helpful alternative thoughts:

Blaming: This is where you blame other people for the pain you feel and the problems you have. Now, people may fuck you over big time, but blaming them for everything that

comes after means making them responsible for all of your choices and decisions for time eternal. That's far too much power to give over to some motherfucker. In reality, you have every right to be your own self-advocate, to make your own choices, and be responsible for your own decisions from here on out.

Times I think this way:

More helpful alternative thoughts:

Shoulds: Dude. If people would just do what I say, the world would be a brilliant place. We all have a list of shoulds for the rest of the world. How people should behave. How they should

treat us. When they don't follow those rules, we get all kinds of legit butthurt. Then we put on our judgy-pants about what they are doing, even when it's shit that we seriously don't even need to be worrying about.

Times I think this way:

More helpful alternative thoughts:

Emotional Reasoning: This is where we presume that whatever emotion we are feeling is an indicator of something fucked up about ourselves. That if we feel something, it must be a fundamental truth. Like, if you feel guilty, you clearly are guilty. And while feelings are real, they don't always correspond to reality. If our thinking is distorted, then our emotional reactions go along for the ride and it becomes a mobius strip of mind-fuckery.

Times I think this way:

More helpful alternative thoughts:

Fallacy of Change: This is the expectation that people should change to make life better for you. And that their changing is what is going to make you happy. Of course, you can always ask people to change. But the only person you can really control is your own damn self. And the choices you make will have far more of an impact on your happiness, because then you can take credit for successes.

Times I think this way:

More helpful alternative thoughts:

Global Labeling: This is the shitty political extremist category of distorted thinking styles. It's all about stereotyping and one dimensionality, as if knowing one thing allows you to know everything. It's what leads to prejudice, relationship issues, and the tendency to make snap judgments.

Times I think this way:

More helpful alternative thoughts:

Being Right: You feel like you have something to prove in every interaction . . . and what you need to prove is your inherent rightness. You are the lawyer, judge, and jury . . . and you aren't hearing anything from the opposition. A different opinion or perspective? INADMISSIBLE! Being right can really fuck up your ability to have caring and reciprocal relationships with others.

Times I think this way:

More helpful alternative thoughts:

Heaven's Reward Fallacy: Heaven's Reward folks totally went to church with my grandma. They are the people who have some kind of sense that if they deny themselves and sacrifice constantly, they are somehow working toward some magical reward because there is a scorecard being kept. This isn't about people who are trying to be better human beings, because that's what we should all do, but a sort of false piety that speaks to paying into the system like it's an investment. It doesn't have to be a literal storing of your treasures in heaven; maybe you are expecting public recognition of your moral superiority. Then, of course, when the reward doesn't come, it sucks pretty bad and creates serious bitterness. What was all the sacrifice for, then? If you aren't doing the right thing with your heart truly in it, you're just depleting yourself without real payoff.

Times I think this way:

More helpful alternative thoughts:

Which thinking errors did you notice you use the most? Which alternatives were the most helpful?

Appreciative Inquiry

In mental health, some of the best communication tools we teach people actually come from the business world, since so much of business is working with other people towards shared goals. This exercise, from *The Five Wisdom Energies: A Buddhist Way of Understanding Personalities, Emotions, and Relationships* by Irini Rockwell is drawn from industrial psychology and is used in companies to build teamwork. It's designed to help us become more conscious of our desires and habitual patterns so we can communicate more effectively.

You can do this exercise on your own, or with someone else. If you complete this exercise with someone else, take turns being the interviewer. You can ask for more information in a positive way ("Oh, wow! I'd love to hear more about that!"), but don't judge, correct, or cross-examine their answers. Do not add your own response until the other person has gone through each question. After the exercise is completed, switch roles, and your partner asks the same questions of you and listens to your answers.

This exercise is meant to help crystalize our longer-term relational goals and the best ways we can support them.

What are the times in your life that you have felt the best about yourself?

What are the times in your life that you have felt the best about your relationships with others?

What outside circumstances helped make these good experiences possible?

What things were other people doing or what qualities did they have that helped create experiences that were good for you?

What things were you doing or what qualities within you helped create these good experiences?

What goals, hopes, and dreams do you have for yourself and for your relationships in the future? What would you like your relationships to look like 5 years from now?

What would you like to see yourself contributing to make that happen?

Questions for Treatment Providers

No matter what treatment strategies you are researching, there is a decent chance you are looking for a treatment provider. Whether it is a prescriber, a professional counselor, an occupational therapist to help you find the best weighted blanket, or a nutritionist to help you adjust your diet and add some supplements.

Lifestyle, medical model, or complementary strategies all have experts that may help your journey. But I swear, some days it feels like 99.44% of the battle is finding a provider who you can get in to see in a reasonable amount of time, really listens, is competent in treating you, and is a real partner in helping you get better.

You may be getting treatment in a community mental health setting, where you don't have much choice in providers, but if you do have choices, finding people who you really connect to and can work well with is important. So here are some things to look for when researching plus a place to take notes on what you found:

What is their license and/or certification? Where did they train? Who provides their practice oversight?

List your specific issues and treatment needs: (eg, anxiety, depression, family of origin issues, relationships troubles, etc)

What do they specialize in? What is their treatment approach? What is their training in your specific issues?

What is their experience in treating your personal treatment needs? Are they comfortable with working with your specific issues?

List any other circumstances you have that could impact your care: (eg, medical conditions or disabilities, prejudices you face, your living situation, your financial situation, etc)

Are they comfortable dealing with these issues?

Are they comfortable working with your other providers?

What do they charge? Are there additional fees for other services? How do they accept payment? Do they take insurance? Do they take HSA cards? Will they give you a superbill for reimbursement?

Can they see you soon, and at a time that works with your schedule?

Questions to Ask Your Prescriber About Medications and Supplements

What symptoms does this medication or supplement treat?

How does it work in the body?

Is this intended for short or long term use?

If it is for short term use what will be our longer term treatment plan?

What side effects could I have from this medication or supplement?

How long will they probably last?

What side effects are dangerous? Which ones mean I should go to an emergency room? Which should I notify you about and how do you want to be notified?

How should I notify you if I want to discuss discontinuing this medication or supplement?

If I no longer want to take this medication will I need to taper off of it?

How long will it take to start working?

Does this medication interact with any other drugs I'm taking?

Does this medication interact with any other supplements or herbs?

What else do you recommend for me to consider in order to help with my symptoms?

Health Log

If you are trying to figure out how your body responds to all of the input it receives, a health journal is your best tool. Now that there is an app for everything, you can make this as easy and digitized as possible if that is your preference. If you are old school, you can just jot down the following every day:

- The meds you are taking, the dosage, and the time (both prescription and OTC)

- Same for any supplements

- What you ate

- What you drank

- Other substances ingested (ahem)

- Vaccines received

- Exercise/movement engaged in

- Hours and quality of your sleep

- Any physical ailments and whatever you used to manage them (asthma attack, back pain)

- Any accidents or injuries.

A lot of docs love if your health journal includes your medical history and your family history as well, so if you are sharing it with them you have it all in one place.

There are a lot of benefits to keeping a health journal. You'll be more organized and streamlined for doctor's appointments and your own personal tracking. You'll save money because you can see your history treatment at a glance. For example, you can go "oh yeah tried that two years ago and it gave me a horrible headache, no thanks." You'll be more likely to figure out food triggers. You'll notice how stressors (lack of sleep, crappy work schedule, people around you being all people-y) are influencing symptoms. And you'll be more likely to figure out what meds/supplements are helping or hindering.

Day/date:

	Meds	Food	Drink	Exercise	Sleep	Pain	Anxiety	Other
Morning								
Midday								
Afternoon								
Evening								
Night								

PART III:
LIVING
WITH YOUR
ANXIETY

C Anxiety (and fear and stress and its other assorted cousins) is necessary for our survival. If it didn't exist we would stroll off the top of parking garages to our deaths pretty immediately. It's not something we want turned off, but we don't want it controlling everything we try to do over. The techniques in this last chapter are all about forging a healthy relationship with your brain so that appropriate anxiety can pass on its messaging to you without it taking control over everything you are trying to accomplish in a given day.

And because social anxiety is a particular bear for a lot of people, I've also included some resources for dealing specifically with the having-to-connect-to-other-people part of life. This part of the book is less about interactive exercises and more about skills you can practice and take with you. Not all of them are going to work for everyone. This is about choosing what works best for you.

An important science-y note about the mindfulness and breathing exercises in this part of the workbook: If trauma is something you're dealing with, be aware that it changes our breathing. When we are out of our zone of tolerance, our breathing becomes shallow (to change oxygen movement throughout the body to prepare for the perceived attack). And trauma survivors often hold their breath regularly without realizing it. And that creates tension and more body dysregulation that we are often even aware of.

We can learn from yoga practitioners who have been developing trauma-informed practices that can help you use mindful movement and breathing for trauma recovery without being retraumatized or triggered by it. David Emerson's trauma-informed yoga is an evidence-based practice for trauma recovery, and there are several unique aspects to how he cues yoga that I use as a teacher and clinician.

One of the biggest differences in his approach is that he doesn't tell practitioners when to breathe in and out. He only suggests noticing it. If you have taken a more traditional yoga class, you'll remember being told when to breathe in and breathe out constantly. That's why the first breathwork exercise in this chapter is designed to help you just notice your breath, with no plan of altering it. Trauma survivors regularly struggle to notice their breathing at all, so beginning to do so is a really big deal. And it helps us notice when we are holding our breath as well. While an anxiety or panic response can include very rapid, shallow breathing, a trauma response may invoke a locked jaw, breath suppression, and abdominal inhibition.

Another really amazing resource is David Treleaven's book Trauma-Sensitive Mindfulness. If you are a trauma survivor or an individual who works with trauma survivors, this book is invaluable. He offers suggestions for managing trauma triggers and activation during mindful meditation practice, which can also be applied to breathwork to help maintain that polyvagal window of tolerance.

- Recognize your internal go and stop signals (thoughts, feelings, body sensations) as markers of how you respond to different breathing techniques. Which are most helpful? Which are activating?

- Take breaks when you need to or alter how you are holding your body. Move into a more comfortable position or wiggle in place a little.

- Open your eyes, if they have been closed.

- Change to slow, mindful breathing if you were trying one of the more complicated pranayama techniques.

- Focus on an external object that is in your line of vision.

- Shorten your breathwork practice period or otherwise adjust the practice itself (for example, the 4-7-8 breathing pattern can be altered to shorter breaths).

Learn and practice breathwork when you are in a relaxed state, rather than trying to do it when you are already activated. The more you practice when your body isn't under siege, the more likely you are at being successful with it when your body is under siege.

Tips and Tricks for Unfucking Your Conversations

I'm not sure when the cool kids started social media shaming the rest of us for having scripts for conversations. Fuck. We're tired, we're overwhelmed, and we are hella anxious... having some tools in our back pocket isn't a bad thing at all, and it's not inauthentic. It means we care enough about other people to plan ahead of time how to authentically connect with them. So here are some starter scripts and other tricks to help your process.

1. Ask open ended questions ("What was _____ like?" will generally carry a conversation further than "Did you like _____?")

2. Don't play smart. Meaning, don't pretend you know something if you don't. Generally, people love sharing what they know so asking them about something is awesome. If you are introduced to someone and they tell you that they do data analysis for a living and you don't know jack-all what that means, totally ask them! Like "I don't know much about that but it sounds like it could encompass a lot of things... I'd love to hear more about what you do." People generally like the opportunity to teach something and learning something new is always a good use of the learner's time (even if it doesn't apply directly to their life in that present moment).

3. Pay attention. Like directly. Don't fiddle with your phone or attend to other things going on in the area... be fully present and listen to understand them rather than to respond.

4. Watch for falling into conversational weeds. If you find yourself going down bunny trails, or are repeating yourself (I do this a lot by habit, because I have to do it as a therapist... and it's not cute when hanging out with friends), or generally rambling? Pull back. Watch for cues that you are starting to lose your audience.

5. Don't equate your experience to theirs. It's a common way of trying to make a connection, especially for people who are neurodiverse (because if you don't neurocept well, you have to adapt to make that connection). But it can lead to the other person feeling like you are trying to redirect the focus to yourself. It's totally cool to just reflect the emotional content of what they are saying. Like "That's amazing!" or "That's fucking awful." Or even just "Wow,

that's a lot to go through." If they ask you about your experience, that's when you can say "Something similar, so I can empathize to a certain extent... but everyone's situation is unique, so I certainly wouldn't assume I know exactly what you are going through and me saying I do would be a pretty dick move."

6. Give authentic compliments. And you know what's interesting? I realized when I moved away from the habit of giving looks-based compliments (since they tend to be so gender presumptive) I gave better compliments in general that made people feel good about themselves as a person, not just how they presented. Like instead of saying "You look so pretty!" I will say something like "I love your look today, you're rocking it!" Yanno? Like saying "your eye make-up is so on point today" will feel so much more authentic to someone who is gender-expansive than "your eye makeup is gorgeous!" and feels just as awesome a compliment to anyone femme.

7. Avoid the question "why." I swear, all human brains immediately answer "I don't know." I don't use why questions as a therapist and my interns and students aren't allowed to either. Seriously, try experimenting with reframing those questions as "how did that work?" or "help me understand what went on there?"

8. Don't get into power struggles. If someone says something that seems super off the wall, just give it back to them. My favorite response to pronouncements that are racist, sexist, or otherwise shitty and othering is to say "Oh! That's not been my experience of .... What has yours been?" Instead of starting an argument, you've giving them back their bullshit with an invitation to explain it.

DEAR MAN

Dialectical Behavior Therapy is a set of skills that blend mindfulness and cognitive-behavioral strategies to help individuals better manage both their internal world while caring for their relationships. It's designed to regulate emotion, be effective interpersonally, center mindfulness, and help you tolerate distress—especially with the people that you care about! DEAR MAN is an acronym for a well-known DBT interpersonal effectiveness skill, meaning it's not necessarily going to increase your effectiveness at getting what you want from someone—which is interpersonal manipulation—but it does help you communicate your read on a situation with clarity and calm.

D stands for *Describe*. This is just the facts of the situation, not how you feel or what you want. It's only "this is my understanding of what's up." e.g. "We've been at this for five hours and we are halfway done."

E stands for *Express*. This is when you share your emotional response, but doing so with accountability by using I statements. Meaning "I feel..." not "You made me feel..." e.g. "I am really getting tired."

A stands for *Assert*. This is how you express what you need or set a boundary firmly and concretely. No hinting or maybe-ing. e.g. "So I'm not going to be able to do this for another five hours."

R stands for *Reinforce*. This is where you show your recognition of your relationship with the other person, demonstrating that you understand reciprocity. It may mean saying "I appreciate that you are so committed and are working so hard to get this done." or "I think it's unfair for me to not have told you this information earlier...because I respect you enough for how to have all of the information."

M stands for *Mindful*. This just means not getting distracted and focusing your attention on the conversation, which demonstrates it's important to you and is respectful of them. e.g. no looking at your phone while you discuss important things.

A stands for *Appear Confident*. This doesn't mean you shouldn't be nervous, but you can be confident in what you're sharing as being important to you and valid. e.g. don't back down on your position if the other party shares a conflicting perspective.

N stands for *Negotiate*. Unless it's a firm boundary, this is a relationship you care about and it's good to consider the other person. What can you give in return? e.g. "I can finish whatever you don't get done tomorrow. I know that's not what you wanted but it's the best that I can do at this time."

Mindfulness Meditation

No saffron robes needed, I promise. But meditation releases dopamine, serotonin, oxytocin, and endorphins. And it's cheaper than Crossfit. 3000 years of Buddhist practice has something going for it, yeah?

Here's my recipe for mindfulness meditation:

Sit upright. If you can do this without back support, like on the floor on a cushion, then good on you. If you need a straight back chair, do that. If you can't sit at all, that's okay, too. Get yourself in whatever position is most comfortable. The reason sitting is better than laying down is that the point is to fall awake, not fall asleep. But the point is also to not be in screaming fucking pain, so don't stress it.

Soft-focus your eyes so they aren't closed but they are seeing without actually seeing. You know what I mean. Be visually spaced out because what you are really going to be paying attention to is inside you.

And now you are going to breathe in and out. And focus on your breath. If you have never done this before it's going to be weird and hard. But for the record, if you have done this a zillion times chances are still good that it will be weird and hard.

If you catch yourself being distracted, just label it "thinking" and go back to focusing on your breath. Thinking isn't a failure in the least. It's gonna happen. And noticing it and bringing the mind back to the present moment is the point. So it's a total win.

Treat your bodily reactions like any other random thought. Itching is common. If you catch yourself itching, label it thinking three times before succumbing to the urge to scratch. You may be surprised at how often your brain is creating things for you to focus on. Of course, if you have real pain, don't ever ignore that. Rearrange yourself for comfort and don't be a hero.

A lot of people feel awful during meditation, thinking they suck at it because they are continuously distracted by chatting thoughts. That's okay. Your brain is desperately seeking to story-tell. All kinds of distracting stuff is going to come up. You are going to think about what you need to cook for dinner. Or a conversation you had at work. Or whether or not you should buy new sneakers or go to a movie this weekend.

I'm not even going to pretend that this shit is easy to do when you are spun up. But it's important to at least try. Because part of a panic attack is the stories our brain starts telling us about the attack itself. And it's generally not a pretty story. The chemicals released during an anxiety or panic attack are designed to get your breathing ramped up and your heart racing. So your brain starts insisting that you are going to have a heart attack or will stop breathing. That's not going to happen. When you catch that thinking, remind yourself that it's a biochemical response, but not reality.

And here is the thing about mindfulness meditation . . . research shows that it disrupts the storytelling process of the default network. We used to think the only way to do that was a distraction by outside events and stimulus, but the opposite works, too.

So keep breathing. The continued, conscious effort to breathe and un-tense will slow the heart rate back down and help you get more oxygen flowing. It's a literal chemical counterbalance. And it gives your brain the space it needs to tell itself new stories.

Meditation on the Soles of the Feet

One mindfulness technique that can help bring you right back into the moment when your SUDs level is skyrocketing is meditating on the soles of the feet. This exercise has been directly associated with assisting in managing anger responses, and it's been found to be extremely effective for neurodiverse people.

Set the scene by finding as calm and relaxing an atmosphere as possible. Even if you can just dim the lighting a bit, it can really help.

• If you are standing, stand in a natural rather than an aggressive posture. If you are sitting, sit comfortably with the soles of your feet flat on the floor

• Breathe naturally and do nothing

• Cast your mind back to an incident that made you very angry. Stay with the anger

• You are feeling angry, and angry thoughts are flowing through your mind. Stay with your anger. Your body may show signs of anger like rapid breathing

• Now, shift all your attention to the soles of your feet

• Slowly, move your toes, feel your shoes covering your feet, feel the texture of your socks or tights, the curve of your arch, and the heels of your feet against the backs of your shoes. If you do not have shoes on, feel the floor, carpet, or ground with the soles of your feet

• Keep breathing naturally and focus on the soles of your feet until you feel calm

• Meditate on the soles of your feet for about ten to fifteen minutes

• Slowly come out of your meditation, sit quietly for a few minutes, and resume your daily activities

•

Deep Breathing

When I work with kids I call it belly breathing. When I work with vets, police officers, and first responders I call it tactical breathing. The official term is diaphragmatic breathing or abdominal breathing which are just the most ridiculous words ever . . . I swear to Buddha, we must make this shit up just to see if we can get people to follow along.

So if you have seen any of those terms it's totally all the same thing. And all it really means is that you are taking in your breaths by contracting your diaphragm, which is a muscle that lies horizontally across your body, between your abdominal cavity and your thoracic cavity.

Sounds complicated? Not so much. You totally know how to take a deep breath. It's when your belly moves instead of your chest. You get far more oxygen in your blood when you are breathing in this manner, which will disrupt the anxiety response. Have you ever been so anxious that you felt light headed and about to pass out? Your breathing was likely totally to blame. You weren't breathing in a way that gave you the oxygen you need to manage your anxiety response.

If you want to practice this, lie down and put something on your belly. Your favorite stuffed animal, your unopened growler bottle, whatever. You should see it move while you breathe.

Yup, that's it, you got it.

Try to focus on your breathing instead of the other bullshit chatter that your brain is insisting you pay attention to. Counting helps, too. Try these counts for breathing in, holding, and breathing out.

Only count as high as you can comfortably go. You aren't gonna get graded on your breathing and it isn't meant to be stressful. If you're asthmatic, have allergies, etc., anything more than 6 seconds may be literally impossible. No sweat, okay?

Breathe In and Count To	Breathe Out and Count To	Hold and Count To
3	3	3
3	3	6
6	6	6
6	6	9
9	9	9
9	9	12
12	12	12

Alternative Nostril Breathing

Sanskrit Name: *Nadi Shodhana*

ALTERNATIVE NOSTRIL BREATHING TECHNIQUE — INHALE — EXHALE

This breathing technique has been shown to calm the body by giving you control of your autonomic function...meaning it literally helps you calm yourself down and has been shown to be more effective for this purpose than other breathing techniques designed for the same purpose (e.g., paced breathing).

To practice ANB, fold your middle three fingers into your palm so only your thumb and pinky finger are extended. This is the universal sign for "call me," the Hawaiian sign for "hang loose," and my alma mater's sign for our mascot, the roadrunner.

Beep, beep.

Ahem, anyway. Use your thumb to close one nostril and breathe in through the other.

Move your hand to use your pinky to close the other nostril while releasing your thumb from the first nostril to breathe out.

Lather, rinse, repeat.

Passive Progressive Relaxation

Now we are going to work on relaxing each part of your body moving progressively down. This isn't one of those exercises where you tense up first so you can then relax yourself and feel the difference. That's a useful exercise on other occasions, but not when you already fucking know you are tense and don't need anything else making you more tense.

If it helps you to have prompts, you can find lots of guided progressive relaxation exercises on YouTube.

Start with the deep breathing. You know how to do this part now, so you can move the teddy bear or growler. Lie down, relax, and lay your arms and hands, palms to the earth, down to your side next to you. Close your eyes if that feels safe and comfortable for you.

- Start at the top of your head. Tune in, beginning with your crown, moving slowly down your scalp. Feel your ears relax.

- Feel your temples relax, and then your brows.

- Feel your eyes relax, then your cheeks, then your nose, and then your mouth. Relax your lips and your tongue.

- Feel your throat relax. Then your neck.

- Feel your shoulders relax. Focus on letting them drop everything they've been holding for you. They get to rest, too.

- Focus on your right hand. Let the calm flow from your right shoulder, down your arm. Through your wrists, then into each finger. Start with your thumb and move through each finger to your pinky, relaxing every digit.

- Now focus on your left hand. Let the calm flow from your left shoulder, down your arm. Through your wrists, then into each finger. Start with your thumb and move through each finger to your pinky.

- Now focus back on your shoulders, and let the relaxation flow through your chest down into your belly. Your belly is moving gently as you continue deep breathing, but otherwise has no other work to do right now. It doesn't have to hold itself up or in with any tightness.

- Go back up to your shoulders, and let the relaxation flow down your upper back to your lower back. You've been holding a lot there, haven't you? Maybe the entirety of the world. You don't have to, at least for right now. Let it go for a while.

- Relax through your buttocks, through your root chakra, and down through your hips. Let the calm flow down through your thighs.

- Move down to your knees, then your calves.

- Move down to your ankles. Your feet. Let yourself relax each toe. Start with your big toe and move to your pinky toe.

Once you feel ready, open your eyes and slowly get back up again. You may feel a little sleepy, or woozy, or fuzzy. That's okay. Take your time rejoining the world and remember what relaxed feels like. You're allowed to feel that way!

Chair Yoga

These are all bend-at-the-waist yoga forms that I specifically use to calm the vagus nerve and get the parasympathetic nervous system back online. Which is a fancy way of saying they can help disrupt the anxiety process.

They are all meant to be done seated. You can absolutely do these poses on a mat, but a chair can give you some good support, especially if you don't have much yoga experience, have limited mobility, some pain issues, etc. But even in a chair, and even when not doing yoga forms that require extending the arms, you can still end up hurting yourself... and yoga is not supposed to hurt.

Some rules:

1. Don't do shit that hurts.

2. Modify whatever you need to modify so it doesn't hurt.

3. Don't do these exercises at 100% effort. Allow yourself the experience of only putting in 10% effort. Yoga works just as well (if not better) at 10% effort. Let yourself relax.

4. If you find yourself holding your breath, you're working too hard. You should be breathing because you are a human being and the breathing in and out thing is important, okay?

5. Use a chair that isn't on wheels, has a straight back, and (ideally) does not have arms.

6. Make sure you tell everyone that you totally did yoga today.

Mountain Pose

Sit straight up and extend your spine.

Root down in your chair on the lowest part of your tailbone (your sit bones)—the two points that take the weight of your body when you sit.

Be mindful to keep your legs at a 90 degree angle, with your knees directly over your ankles, with some space between your knees. This is a great pose to simply engage your core, check in with your posture, and focus on your breath. Come to this pose after each of the poses below.

Roll your shoulders back and pull your belly in toward your spine, then relax your arms down at your sides.

Cat-Cows

Keeping both feet on the floor and your spine long, put your hands on the tops of your thighs, or your knees if you can do so comfortably.

Arch your spine and roll your shoulders toward your back. Moo!

Round your spine, and drop your chin toward your chest, rolling your shoulders forward inward to your chest. Meow!

Continue moving back and forth between cat and cow positions, experimenting with moving during inhalations and exhalations, 5 to 10 cycles.

Sufi Rolls

As you inhale, lean your torso over to the right and then circle it out in front of you and around to the left, coming around the back as you exhale. Create a circle, leading from the belly button. Inhale forward and exhale backward. Then reverse.

Chair Pigeons

Move back into seated mountain, then bring your right ankle up to rest on your left thigh. Keep your knee parallel with your ankle as much as possible and hold this form for 5 breath cycles if you can do so without pain or discomfort. If you want to deepen the stretch, you can bend your waist forward over your leg. Repeat with the left leg.

Seated Forward Bend

Start back in seated mountain form, then fold your upper body over your legs from the waist. You can leave your hands at your sides or use them for extra support in the form by resting them on your thighs, then sliding them down your legs as you hinge forward. Experiment with holding this form for 5-10 cycles of breathing. When you are ready, move back into seated mountain form.

Single-Leg Stretch

For this one, you can scooch forward closer to the edge of the chair for more traction (but not so close you end up biffing it, okay?)

Stretch your right leg out, pointing your toes up and resting your heel on the floor. Rest your hands on your right leg, then lift up through your spine and bend over your right leg, sliding your hands down your leg to support your movement forward. You can take the stretch as far as it feels comfortable, but don't push yourself to the place of pain. You can hold onto your ankle or the back of your calf for support if you are able to drop that low. Hold this position for 5 breath cycles, if possible, and experiment with deepening the pose as you breathe.

Repeat with your left leg.

Final Relaxation Form

Sitting comfortably in your chair, drop all muscle tension. Close your eyes or allow your gaze to soft focus into the middle distance. Focus on your breath and notice sensations in your body. Allow yourself 2-3 minutes of rest before getting up from your practice.

Meditation and Breathing Log

Here's a place to keep track of the mindfulness, meditation, breathing, movement, and relaxation techniques you are trying and their effectiveness. Keeping track like this is especially helpful when your brain wants to act super hopeless about everything and you need a reminder that you are making good progress and not wasting your time.

Technique	SUDs before	SUDs after	Notes

CHECKING IN BEFORE HEADING OUT

Workbooks like this aren't easy. There's a ton of emotional junk to haul out and healing to do, so you're a high-key bad ass for doing it. But instead of just saying "go you!" I want you to really see the effects of the work you just did. If you were in my office I could say "Hey, look at how you handled that versus three months ago, that's amazing!" but since you aren't here for me to just tell you, we gotta do just one more worksheet so I can show you.

Becoming skillful in the management of our emotions is not a recipe. If it was, we'd all follow the recipe and everyone would have a lovely homemade flan of a calm life. Instead, we have to test a lot of different stuff out and find what works best for us. It's tough work. Took a while to get fucked, takes a while to get unfucked. Checking in on your progress is really helpful in not getting overwhelmed and dissuaded from continuing to work at it. So let's check in now that you've done a bunch of the exercises in this workbook.

What did you learn about yourself through this process?

Which skills were the most helpful?

In what ways?

Are you finding that you have better skills to navigate your anxiety than you had in the past?

Do you believe that you have more control over your emotions that you had in the past?

Are certain skills becoming easier to access and utilize once you are activated? Do you see the potential for them becoming second nature?

Are you finding that anxiety's grip on you is getting tighter or looser?

Are you finding yourself more or less activated by situations that made you anxious in the past? Are there differences in the level of anxiety or the number of instances of anxiety?

What's next for you?

FURTHER READING

Why Zebras Don't Get Ulcers by Robert Sapolsky

This book is totally about the body as a biological machine and explains why humans are more susceptible to stress-related diseases (like, you know, anxiety) than animals are. The last chapter is more self-help oriented. But if you like to nerd out on the science part, this book is the schizz. (Sapolosky is also heavily featured in the National Geographic documentary "Stress: Portrait of a Killer." Last time I looked, it was up on YouTube.)

The Meaning of Anxiety by Rollo May

May was smart AF, y'all. And an amazing philosopher as well as a clinician. I think he missed out on many of the ways lack of privilege can affect anxiety, but it doesn't mean that many of his ideas weren't brilliant and a good starting place. And hey, he was a well-educated, well off white dude in the middle 20th century, so not exactly an intersectional feminist (and, TBF, relational cultural theory didn't even exist yet) so I give him a pass on that end. It's still a good grounding if you are interested in the historical underpinnings of anxiety.

Toward a New Psychology of Women by Jean Baker Miller

Jean Baker Miller's theories about mental health looked at how stereotypes have shaped mental illness. She took what all of the institutional ideas about power, success, strength, and autonomy really mean and turned them on their head.

In a Different Voice by Carol Gilligan

Gillian's work molded neatly with that of Miller's, even though they were not working together at the time they were researching and writing these books. Gilligan was focused on looking at human development through a new lens, instead of only the current theories available regarding mental health. Her interest was in the space that lies between experience and thought, and how those things shape and inform each other. Her use of the word "voice" to replace the notion of "selfhood" is something that I have carried forward in my own research.

Learned Optimism by Martin Seligman

If we can learn helplessness, we can learn the reverse, right? Fuck yeah, that's right! Human beings are wired to the negative as a protective mechanism that doesn't serve us super well in the long run. Seligman uses classic cognitive therapy techniques with a twist to show people how to rewire their brains into more positive thinking and responses.

Furiously Happy: A Funny Book About Horrible Things by Jenny Lawson

Jenny Lawson (The Bloggess) writes about surviving the whole host of disorders she has struggled with, including depression and anxiety. She walks that balance of not taking it all so seriously and taking it very very seriously. It's a fine line, isn't it? She does the thing. This makes it possible to laugh and relate and actually feel better without disrespecting the seriousness of what you're going through.

First We Make The Beast Beautiful by Sarah Wilson

Sarah Wilson's personal journey with anxiety led her to do tons of research and interviews and share the things that she has found the most helpful. Like Jenny Lawson, Sarah writes her reality with no filters so you can see the good, bad, and ugly.

The Upside of Stress by Kelly McGonigal

The stress cycle in and of itself is not a bad thing. This book shows all the research in how the perception of stress feeds our response to it and the impact it has on our bodies.

Burnout by Emily Nagoski and Amelia Nagoski

This book is specific to the stress cycle and overwhelm experienced by women in this culture, some of which I touched on in this book. This book uses a lot of science and empathy to help you understand and work through your biological stress cycle, plus tips on tapping out from cultural standards (such as needing to have a perfect body) that make all of these issues worse.

The Gift of Fear (And Other Survival Signals That Protect Us From Violence) by Gavin de Beker

Hear me out. I want you to have a life with as little anxiety as possible. But I want you to experience fear as a very real emotion that you should listen to and respond to. Gavin de Beker writes about how we ignore those very important bodily signals that something is not right and covers the science of how fear works and why we should pay heed to it.

Notes on a Nervous Planet by Matt Haig

I consider this book the Rollo May of the 21st century, it really speaks to how society feeds anxiety which we always, always, always need to take into account when working through our own issues. The personal is political and the political is personal.